Tyrone Lewis (he/him) is a UK Poe
Poetry Slam champion, Axis Po
of debut collection Blackish.

Tyrone is the founder of Proc___ _____ __ ____ __ ___
monthly spoken word night Process. He was also one of the
inaugural Albany Associate Artists. As well as performing,
Tyrone is known for hosting, producing and featuring at many
spoken word nights across the UK.

Tyrone has also been involved with a number of major national
poetry events over the years including 2010's Word Cup, 2012's
Shake the Dust and 2015's Shot from the Lip, as well as helping
out with UniSlam since 2016.

Away from poetry, Tyrone is a full-time senior video editor.
Tyrone has become known across the UK not only for his writing
and performance but also for his work behind a camera.

*'When I think about poets who will make new people fall in
love with spoken word, I think about Tyrone.'*
@websterpoet/@SabotageReviews

'Jedi grand master poet.' @SpitTheAtom

'Vanguard of the spoken word community.' @RepeatBeatPoet

'Legendary creature.' @StandUpPoet

2 Black 2 Furious

Tyrone Lewis

Burning Eye

BurningEyeBooks
Never Knowingly
Mainstream

This edition published by Burning Eye Books 2023

www.burningeye.co.uk

@burningeyebooks

Burning Eye Books
15 West Hill, Portishead, BS20 6LG

ISBN 978-1-913958-39-8

Printed and bound by CPI Group (UK) Ltd, Croydon, CR0 4YY

Dedicated to CazAnn Moy.

Always has been, always will be.
Just had to make it official this time around.

*Whilst this book is officially titled 2 Black 2 Furious,
the spiritual name for this book is:*

Blackish 2:
Electric Boogaloo

Contents

Blackish 2: Electric Boogaloo

after 'Blackish' by Tyrone Lewis

The public demanded that
we do a sequel.
Saw the reactions to the first poem
and conceded that
even if the second one isn't as good
the profit margins could be better.

They gave us more budget
for the second poem.
This time
there's
even
more
line
breaks.

We've added more
stanzas too.

Kept the length
changing
so the poem's pacing
keeps you

on
your
toes.

The CGI has improved
so you can't tell the metaphors
from reality.
The publishers saw
potential in my racial conflict.
Deemed it a viable franchise
with spin-off
and merchandising potential.

This time it's Blacker.

We don't know what that means either
but we know that there's more
gratuitous cameos
in this one.
We dug up Trayvon and George,
Breonna and Damilola
'cause we know that shit sells.
Audiences responded well to the trauma
in the first one
so we mined
more of that for you this time around
then stuck in Chris Pratt
for the star power.

We're going to mention Meghan Markle in this one
just to piss off Clarkson and Morgan.
Figured it'd be controversial enough to get us
a full half-hour as the lead topic
on the Jeremy Vine show
with callers debating over
just how racist this poem is.

We'll let the Black guy survive this one.

Studio wanted to make sure
a trilogy was still possible
but we're warning you not to get attached
to the supporting cast.
There's only so many Black characters we can feature
in a mainstream poem.

Publishers said they had to make sure
this poem stands out from the crowd
so they're only putting out one Black poem
in this quarter. Their release schedule can't
possibly have two.

If this poem is profitable, then the next one
can feature Black joy.
We need to see the financial returns
before we try to make that canon.

Welcome to the Real World

To this day, I'm still disappointed that
my mornings don't begin with an over-the-top
title sequence. My life still doesn't come
with an opening theme tune
and I'm still getting to grips with that.

There are no recaps.
No *previously ons*.
I'm not reminded of my past storylines that
might come into play
in the next twenty-four hours.

My life is not a tightly written narrative.

There's no room for ad breaks
and I've still not been afforded the creative freedom
that comes with streaming.

I'm still trying to figure out
who the season regulars are.
Who's recurring and who's guest starring.

I'm just about keeping track of
what channel I'm on.
I'm just about coping with
being live.

No one has told me how many seasons I've got
before cancellation.
I'm just hoping I resolve all my plot threads
before the credits roll.

2 Black 2 Furious

This poem is so Black
it was being racially profiled
before I even wrote it.
This poem was being overlooked for jobs
despite having all the relevant qualifications
and experience.
This poem is pretty
for a Black poem.
This poem has curves
and an ass.
This poem is so Black
it has cornrows
and dreadlocks
and an afro
and extensions
and a weave.
This poem exclusively eats
jerk chicken
and plantain
and just drinks orange soda
and rum
and ginger beer.
This poem is so Black
a police officer murdered it on video.

This poem is so Black
it comes from the country of Africa.
This poem is so Black
it comes from the country of the Caribbean.
This poem is so Black
its middle name is the N word.
This poem is so Black
that we can't pronounce its real name
so we're just going to call it Kevin.
This poem is so Black
Scarlett Johansson wants to play it in the biopic.

This poem loves anime.
Specifically Naruto and Dragonball Z.
This poem's favourite superhero film
is Black Panther
and everyone mentions
Get Out to this poem.
This poem is so Black
a police officer murdered it on video
and now it's trending on Twitter.

This poem is so Black
people are surprised it likes country music.
This poem can play bass.
This poem is good at sprinting.
This poem is good at basketball.
This poem is good at long-distance running.
This poem can't swim.
This poem is so Black
its dad left it.
This poem is angry.
This poem is mad.
This poem is a thug.
This poem used to be in a gang.
This poem always carries a knife with it.
This poem is so Black
it keeps being asked to be
the one Black poem in a set.
This poem makes most of its money
during Black History Month.
This poem is so Black
a police officer murdered it on video
and now it's trending on Twitter
and now people are protesting.

This poem is so Black
it was killed before it could...

Pain & Gain

I don't go to the gym much.
I feel like carrying the history of my people on my back
gives me enough of a workout.

I sweat a lot
thanks to the fear of letting them down.

I know that if I fail,
we fail.
I know that if they succeed
then they'll ask why I haven't.
I know no matter what I do,
I'll always do it Black.
The variations are if they add in
my single-parent mother
or my low-class background.

I like being alone
as they're the days I don't have to
be.

Not Another Race Poem

Gunshot.
And all we know to do is run.
We run. We sprint.
Nothing else matters right now.
There's screams all around us,
red under our feet.
We run. We sprint.
Our African and Caribbean blood
desperately pumping around our bodies.
Sweat dripping from us.
We're trying to breathe.
Can't breathe.
We run. We sprint.
50m. 75m.
We run. We sprint.
100m. 150m.
We run. We sprint.
And I can't see them anymore.
I've lost them behind me in the noise.
I've lost them behind me in the madness.
I've lost them behind me.
175m and I'm finding pace
I never knew I had.
I need it.
200m.
And I stop.
I can hear the cheering.
It's over; I've won.
A second later
five other year tens follow me
over the finish line.

Kill Your Darlings

The Lord Vader's Prayer

Our Father, who art on the Death Star,
Vader be thy name.
Thy Republic come;
thy will be done
on Hoth as it is on Endor.
Give us this Han who did shoot first
and forgive us our Gunganing
as we forgive those who Jar Jar against us.
And lead us not to the dark side,
but deliver us from the Sith.
For thine is the Jedi,
the power and the force
for ever and ever.

Amen.

Christian Realness

Glory to Jinkx in the highest,
and peace to Bianca in hell.
Raja, heavenly queen.
Almighty Ru, our Mother.
We worship you.
We give you thanks.
We judge you for some dollars.
Lord Michelle Visage,
only bitch of the mother.
Lord Ru, Mama Ru,
you sashay away, the queens of the world.
Have mercy on us.
You are seated at the right hand of the Carson
and Ross Matthews
for Ru alone is the holy one,
Ru alone is the Lord,
Ru alone is the Most High.
Courtney Act, with the holy Katya
in the glory of Bob the Drag Queen.

Amen.

Say I'm Your Best Friend

There never was an explosion.
There were no burns to nurse
in our fallout. No bones I had to let heal.
We left all our memories intact.

I still have *Enchanted* and
an all-nighter we spent watching Disney films
then taking selfies
before we knew that was a thing.

There are no dates we can engrave onto our tombstone.
If pressed,
I can find our birth in Tumblr posts
and Facebook messages,
but our death,

our death is somewhere in a breakup.
Mine, not yours.

It's in the aftershock.
A friendship that couldn't
hide from the quakes.
We were a building that stood standing after impact
but left barren in the aftermath.

There is no bitterness.
I wish there was.
Instead our friendship just…
finished.

You'd always asked me to write a poem about you.
I finally have now.

Bound for Glory

One day you'll write a poem about me.
I hope I don't make it easy for you.
I hope the words
don't come naturally.
I want you to search for them.
Try to pick them out
from the plethora of us.
I want them
to bare your exhausted sweat.
Be the gold reward
you dug deep for with your fingernails.
A shovel is not an option.

I want them to matter.
I want to know we mattered.
I want your words to be coated in emotions.
I'm not even that fussed about which ones;
I just want them to weigh you down.

When you perform it,
don't hide the crack in your voice.
Let it tremble
at our importance
and buckle at our significance.
I hope you split the room.
Put so much of us out in the air that
people latch on to different aspects.
Let them hate me for
genuinely thinking *Back to the Future*
is kind of shit
whilst they can hate you
for never seeing a 'Star War'.

One day you'll write a poem about me
and I hope it causes arguments.

I hope I hate how true it is.
Hate how much of me you
were able to consolidate into the alphabet.
I want it to inspire me
to write a response.
I want it to inspire others.
Motivate them to wipe off the cobwebs
on the filing cabinets in their minds
and relive their pasts.

One day you'll write a poem about me
and I hope it wins slams.
Cuts judges and audiences so raw
that if anyone dares give you less than a nine for it
it's met with a resounding chorus of boos
even if the scoring is only out of five.
I hope it causes a standing ovation
every night.
Including at relaxed performances.

I hope it drags people from the streets
into whatever bar, function room,
former gay club, converted church
or underground hall you're performing in.
I want it to be the poem poets share
with their non-poetry friends
as an example of really good poetry
and a reason why they should
get into this scene.

I want you to write a poem about me.
And this isn't born of narcissism.
(Not entirely, anyway.)
I just want to know
I've affected someone's life.

One day I hope you'll write a poem about me.
An ode or a sonnet.
I'd settle for a haiku.
I hope it's good.
I'd love to hear it one day.

I Am Not a Slam Poet

Chapter One

I am not a 'slam poet'.
I was not birthed onto this stage,
nor am I phoenix
flapping image wings
as my fiery tongue burns your ears.
I am not a political rant in human form.
I am not liberal enough to labour you with
opinions I haven't matured into
potent propaganda
dressed in stanzas,
nor have I lived long enough
that I could potentially bluff
any of that... stuff.
I am not sufficiently wise enough
that I could mould your thoughts,
nor am I innovative enough
to inspire you,
so I'll conserve those thoughts for now.

Chapter Two

I am not American,
nor is my accent
influenced by them.
It remains mine with no
twang added to it.
EMPHASIS
is not drawn out.
SHOUTS
are few and far between.
SEE,
I have not used Icarus's wings
to fly across the blue.
I never got too close to their sun.
And whilst I've swum in YouTube videos of Def Jam

and Button Poetry,
I've not swallowed enough of the water
that my lungs
have been suffocated by their verses.

Chapter Three

I am not dramatic.
I am not 1
enough with my poem 2
act it out, nor do I feel 3
enough 4
me to fully perform.

Chapter Four

I have not practised my art.
My tempo's
erratic.

My stanzas too

diverse.

I need to rehearse my flow
and plan where to go
and not drop in random rhyme
so sublime
it'll stick like classroom chewing gum
in the back of your mind.
I just need better lines.

Chapter ~~Six~~ Five

I make mistakes.
My humanity is apparent.
Omnipotence is not a talent I possess,
nor have my words
created any form of worship.

I don't believe that there's a slam poet.
I don't believe that there's a performance poet,
a written poet,
a poet who only performs on a Tuesday.
I believe in poetry.
In a poet who writes an idea on their phone
they promise they'll expand on later.
I believe in the poet working part-time
using their break to prepare
for their next open mic
and the poet who sits
in their bedroom
with a blank Word document waiting for
inspiration.
I believe in poetry
and the person who takes
photos of landscapes they call poetic.
In those that promote all their events via Facebook and Insta.
I believe in those with work in their notebooks
no other eyes have
or will see.
I believe in poetry,
and any disciple who chooses to follow her
in whatever way, shape or form
is simply…
a poet.

Talking Heads

My poem's telling me
it doesn't want to be too long.
It's too tired for that.
Says it doesn't want to be burdened
with the weight of the world.
Says today is not the day for death.

I offer it love and it shrugs.
Says it guesses
but thought we had
more originality than that.

I ask my poem what it wants.
It asks me to step aside
and writes itself.

Major!

after 'Modern Major-General' by Gilbert and Sullivan

I am the very model of
a poet individual.
My poetry is topical,
political and whimsical.
I know the slams of England
and for open mics, a lot of 'em,
from Hit the Ode to Lovely Word
and Grizzly Pear in Birmingham.

I'm very good with references;
my use of them is clinical.
A true pop culture powerhouse,
I'm at the top, the pinnacle.
It's like an art form of its own.
Tell Angela I am the boss.
Like Tina said, simply the best.
The best like no one ever was.

I'm really good at feature sets
and headlining a lot of nights
with poetry that's virtuous,
that aims to change wrongs into rights.
In short, in matters topical,
political and whimsical
I am the very model
of a poet individual.

I know our poet history;
there's Tennyson and William Blake.
I know the modern torchbearers.
I know the Apple and the Snake.
I'm quite abreast of reading books,
so many poets I have read
whose poetry will stick with me.
Their words will never leave my head.

My poetry is humorous
but then sometimes can make you cry.
I love to hear your oohs and aahs.
I love when tears fall from your eyes.
My serpent tongue can turn a phrase
right into something sinister.
I do highbrow but simple too,
so yeah, fuck the Prime Minister.

Then I can write my debut book
and publish it with Burning Eye
and in it talk of Kanye West,
then tell you just how Black am I.
In short, in matters topical,
political and whimsical
I am the very model of
a poet individual.

In fact, when I know what is meant
by *enjambment* and *iambic*.
When I can bust out lines I know
will always make the people click.
When I can take a commission
and just complete it in my stride.
(You'd think I'd been on TV like
those poets picked for Nationwide.)

When I have learnt what progress
has been made in modern publishing.
When I can go and work the crowd
like I am in a wrestling ring.
In short, when I've a smorgasbord
of literary strategy,
you'll say I am iconic
like I am 'Bohemian Rhapsody'.

For my vast poetic knowledge
(though it's geeky on the nerdy side)
has only helped a little bit,
I've still always enjoyed the ride.
You see, in matters topical,
political and whimsical
I am the very model of
a poet individual.

The One with Friends

This is a found poem. All the words are from Friends *episode titles.*

Friends with Candy Hearts. The Joke Guy
and the Dirty Girl. Friends
Who Run, Who Nap, Who Party!
Friends with the Routine Where They Got High and
They're Up All Night.
Friends with the Secret Cooking Class
and Hypnosis Tape.
Friends with All the Poker.
Friends with Steaks and Lasagnes.

Friends Who Cry.
Friends with the Inappropriate Joke,
the Inappropriate Laugh. Friends
Where They Can't Remember Last Night.
Friends Who Can't Flirt and the
Inadvertent Kiss… Twice.
Friends Who Flashback to…

the One Where It All Began.
With the Ski Trip, the Bullies, the Jealousy.
Flashback to Ballroom Dancing
and All the Rugby
and All the Football.

To the Wedding, to the Halloween Party
with Princess Leia, George Stephanopoulos,
the Monkey, Underdog, the Evil Orthodontist,
the Ultimate Fighting Champion
and the Holiday Armadillo.

Flashback to London
and the Worst Best Man Ever
with the Free Porn and Where the Stripper Cries.
Flashback to Vegas.
To After Vegas.
To the Rumour, to Barbados.
To Tulsa, to Poughkeepsie,
to…

Friends Who Date.
Friends Who Kiss.
Friends with All the Kissing.
Friends Who… You Know.

Friends with the Fertility Test.
With the Uterus, the Embryos,
with the Sonogram at the End, with the Birth.
With Breast Milk, with the Male Nanny and the Baby on
the Bus.
And Friends Who Go Back to Work.

Friends Where No One Proposes
and the Ick Factor
and the New Crush.
Friends Who Take a Break.
A Big Break.

Friends That Could Have Been…
Friends Where They Can't…
Friends with Denial.
The One Where *Friends* Ends.
The One Where *Friends* Dies.

It's That

It's that twisting of your stomach.
That mind-racing,
sweat-inducing feeling
every time they message you. That
goofy, too big for your face,
more teeth on show than you'd like smile
right after they've looked at you.
It's that, oh my God they touched me
and that wasn't just an accidental meeting of our flesh,
that was an
honest to God
on purpose
form of touching.
It's the wondering.

If they like you,
why they like you,
what to do if they like you,
what to do if they don't like you,
why don't they like you,
do you even like you,
if you don't even like you, why on Earth would they like you,
do you really like them?
Will you ever really like them?
Will you ever really like you?
Will anyone really like you?
Oh God, everyone hates you.
Oh God, they hate you.
Oh God, you hate you. It's

craving more conversations between you
so you can discover more about them and
be astonished at how wonderful they are. It's
how sweet their name tastes so you can't
help but spice up conversations
seasoning them in. It's that moment when
you start entertaining the idea that
they aren't just another person. It's Netflix

and cinemas and two-person selfies.
Walks in the park and 2am McDonald's.
It's willing to admit to them
you've got Little Mix songs on your phone
and that you're not completely against One Direction.
It's when they then buy you a One Direction cake for your birthday
and you give that goofy,
too big for your face,
more teeth on show than you'd like smile
and they give you that same smile back
and they wear it beautifully.

It's that
Han Solo and Leia,
Clark Kent and Lois Lane.
Rachel and Ross,
Buffy and Angel
(or Spike if you're that way inclined).
It's *South Park* and fart jokes.
It's Disney and musicals,
it's Bert and Ernie.
It's that crystallising cheesy moment,
music and tears optional,
where you get...
that feeling.

It's sappy, it's cheesy
and you don't care at all because
it's love.

West Hampstead

I'm sixteen and so are you.
Each of us are doing our
best impressions of human beings
on this Overground train
to West Hampstead.
You're clutching a cake tin
close to your stomach in your left.
Your right is developing a firmer grip
on my arm as we adjust
to the shakes of the train.
I've got two more stops
and a seven-minute walk to your front door left
to figure out how to say
I like you.

It took me the past six hours
and five stops to realise this.
Somewhere in between finding out
your favourite film is *Toy Story 2*
and learning that the scar on your left arm
was from when you and your sister
fought over who loved
AJ from the Backstreet Boys more,
I started to like you.

Our carriage jerks to a stop.
Your right growing tighter
on my arm
as the train forces you a couple steps
closer to me.
Our eyes catch
and we hold this look for longer than is
platonically acceptable.
You force your head to look away first
as my head forces me back nine hours
to when your name was just *Jess's Sister.*

She was still relatively sober when she
forced our paths to cross.
It'd take a couple more hours for her
two extra years of life experiences to fully
kick in.
During her tipsy stage,
she let loose an alcohol-laced warning
that I couldn't have any fun with you
as I started to transition from
plus-one at this party
to Jess's Sister's Carer.

We spent the day in the playground
getting familiar with dirt again.
Competing with each other
to see who could act the youngest.
You won.

We stole the swings and made them our seats,
dragging our feet over tarmac
as our conversations swung from
which of the kids on the roundabout
you most wanted to adopt
to how tired you'd grown of your sister.

Your grip tightens again as our train coughs,
then stutters into life.
One stop left
and I'm noticing how well
your brown hair frames your face,
one strand of it kissing
the corner of your smile.
I can still smell the park on us.

The train doors open.
We're at West Hampstead.
You lead.
I follow you down the platform.

It's just us.

I want to tell you.
I know this would be the time to tell you.
I can see me telling you.
I can see me holding your hand.
I can see my mouth moving.
I can see your eyes looking at mine.
I can see it all
but my body never gets the message.
The words never come.
We just walk
and I know this will be it for us.

We'll meet again,
talk more
and still be friends.
We'll hang out,
have fun
and still be friends.
We'll reveal secrets.
Talk dating woes.
You'll say any girl would be lucky to have me
and we'd still be…

You say you like me.
I don't remember the exact words,
but I can still see you,
clutching the empty cake tin
close to your stomach
with both hands now.
Your hair's still framing your face
with one strand kissing the corner
of your smile.
You still smell like the park.

I hug you goodbye
as I leave you at your front door.
You seem content with the silence
as I hear your sister's warning,
alcohol and all,
whispering on repeat in the back of my head.

It's been fifteen years
and her warning alarm clocks
in my head with such regularity.
Adopts every date,
every friend,
every person
into her family.
Reminds me that I am not there
to have fun with you.
I am not there to have
fun.

High School Never Ends

That's great;
it starts with REM.
We sit around the library table
sharing my headphones.
Next, 'One Week' finishes.
No one owns to up liking the Barenaked Ladies
but no one stopped the song.
Smash Mouth bursts out,
wooden doors swinging on their hinges as
we're All Stars
listening to my mum's MP3
during our lunch break.
It can hold up to 128 MBs of songs,
so we've put everything on it.
Today, we're literally the coolest kids in year ten.
Bowling for Soup plays next.

Wait for It

It's 6.58 in Warren Street.
He's standing here looking down at his shoes;
they haven't shone in a while.
His laces are done up on his left foot
and tucked in on the right.
His trouser cuffs are starting to fray at the bottom.
He kept saying he needed a new pair but
his trousers fit him perfectly.

I think he's wearing a belt.
Either that or his watch kept hitting the button on his
trousers.
There's something metallic near his stomach for sure.
I can't see, though, as his T-shirt is covering it.
It's the only black one he has.
Apparently, most of his others are in the wash.
He apologised. I don't mind.
This one fits him better anyway.

I appreciate him giving me his jacket
but can see the hint of regret hidden behind his eyes.
His dark blue eyes.
I can see the storm he holds in them,
each streak of lighting firing out of his cloudy pupil.

My top's too tight for me.
My jeans are three years old
and hips haven't grown lately.
I felt them tremble when he touched them.
He did it on purpose this time.

My Converse are tired of dancing.
They're hiding feet tapped with bruises
but with toes strong enough to raise me up into
elegance.
I'm on them,

my soles rejecting the ground
as I wait to see what words he wants to form.
As I wait to see if I can survive what he 'wants to tell me'.
As I wait to see if at 6.59pm in Warren Street
I'll still be smiling.

Skater Boy

after 'Sk8er Boi' by Avril Lavigne

He was a Black boy.
Five foot ten but claimed
he's closer to six.
She was six foot.
She was a White girl.
Held English in her throat
but laced it with Scottish.
Could swap in French
at a moment's notice
but at home she was German.
He was just English.
He was a Tottenham fan.
She was a Dortmund fan.
Can I make it any more obvious?

He was a video editor/
poet/photographer/videographer.
She was unemployed
but equipped with a biology degree.
He asked her out,
took her to one of his favourite pubs
in Camden.
She doesn't drink alcohol
but they stayed there till
the pub kicked them out at closing time.
She asked him out for their second date.
They kept dating.
He fell in love with her.
He thought he fell in love with her.
Took him four months to think it.
Five months to say it.
She said it back.
Can I make it any more obvious?

He watched *Firefly* with her.
He asked if she wanted to do

a couple's costume for Halloween.
She said yes.
He dressed as Wash
She dressed as Zoe.
He bought her a Funko Pop of Zoe
for her birthday.
She bought him a nice watch for his.
He never wears watches.
Can I make it any more obvious?

She got employed.
He was still employed.
He kept planning dates with her.
He kept making dates with her.
She kept going on dates with him.

He kept planning dates with her.
He kept making dates with her.
She kept going on dates with him.

He kept planning dates with her.
He kept making dates with her.

He kept planning dates with her.
He kept making dates with her.

He kept planning dates with her.

He kept planning dates with her.

He thought they had communication issues.
He kept trying to bring it up, but…
Can I make it any more obvious?

He doesn't like writing poems about her
but she keeps haunting them.
He keeps tapings of their
relationship's obituary
lined around the backstage of his mind.

He found and replaced
all mentions of her name
and changed them to just say ex
but he can't get rid of her face.
He used to like her face,
used to see her face constantly.
She is no longer his friend on
Facebook.
She no longer talks to him.
She ended things with him.
She does not write poems about him,
he thinks.
She does not think about him,
he thinks.

Can I make it any more obvious?

When Harry Dumped Sally

I wanted that fairytale breakup.
That movie breakup.
That fictional breakup.
I wanted that over-the-top,
that fighting,
that verbal,
that saying things you'll regret breakup.
I wanted that mean breakup.
That emotional,
that I'm in tears,
I'm re-evaluating my life choices,
that too painful to talk about it breakup.
I wanted us to make a scene.
I wanted double-takes,
gasps of breath.
I wanted alcohol in my face,
my clothes ripped to pieces.
I wanted to be held back.
I wanted someone to hold you back.
I wanted a story in the Metro the next day about us.
I wanted a Fringe show out of it.

I wanted a breakup that meant something.

We ended things on a Friday,
I think.
There weren't any raised voices
or broken objects.
Just relief
that we didn't have to pretend
we were in love
anymore.

Horrible History

You're still there in saved memes
and 4pm thoughts. In muscle memory
of cuddles. A holding pattern.
I can still trace the imprint of you
on what was your side of the bed.
You're more echo than longing.
State of fact rather than grief.
I know I loved you, but nowadays
I need the history books to remind me why.

From Buoys II Lads

brotherhood
/ ˈbrʌðəhʊd /
noun

1.
An association of idiots
who will not object when you
tell them we're going to watch
Cats (2019) in cinema.
A community who will laugh
when Judi Dench breaks the
fourth wall to tell you
definitively
that a cat is not a dog.

2.
Truth sayers who mean it
when they say you deserve better
but will not interfere
unless you ask.
You will regret not taking their
advice more often
but you cannot let them
know that.

3.
Brothers related
in *Dungeons & Dragons*
and *Fast & Furious*.
There is no epic tale of
how you all met. No meetcute
you've all rehearsed
that you roll out regularly.
How was never important
for you.

4.
No version of your future
is without them.
Friends doesn't truly bear the
weight of their significance
as they ride or die down the
Cuban mile of your life,
Wiz Khalifa providing the tunes,
Dodge Chargers charging
as you all keep moving forward,
a quarter mile at a time.

Sonnet F9: Tokyo Drift

Two drivers, both alike in quality,
now with Corona placed in every scene.
From street race grudge births a civility
where diesel blood makes Diesel's hands unclean.
So fast, furious nature of these two foes.
A pair of street race legends ride or die,
whose misadventures The Rock overthrows,
complete with Jason Statham driving by.
The nine-part story of their death-marked love
and the continuance of audience eyes,
which, but a financial flop, naught could remove,
is now a mega-successful franchise,
the likes of which the world must all attend,
where here we'll see where race war roads can end.

A thrilling tale this movie with it brings.
The cars, John Cena, fans met with such bliss.
The emotions that Charlie Puth doth sing.
Some may call it stupid, some ludicrous.
For never was a film of more woe
than this of O'Conner and his Toretto.

The Red Light

I remember car horns
and swear words.
I want to say my voice was
drowned out by traffic
but I think you hostaged it
as you ran into the road.
This wasn't the first time you made me think of you
in the past tense.

For a moment
you turned into a eulogy.
Turned into dropped grocery bags
and flowers left underneath your picture
but the car carried on,
you carried on,
we carried on.
And now I carry on
hearing ambulances whenever I think of you.
I keep wondering if someone will ask me
to write about you.
If they'll mention you in the past tense.

His Conscience Comes Into Play

You'll think you know what Death means at twelve.
When they tell you that Nan has passed,
you'll say you understand.
You'll season sentences with words like
grief and *mourning*
as if you know what they taste like.
You'll logic your way into believing that
the confusion in your heart is just
other feelings playing pretend.
You won't remember the funeral
but there's not much you
remember from twelve
so you won't learn guilt. Yet.

You'll see your uncle die in a text message
you receive in a year twelve maths class.
You'll logic that algebra is easier to focus on
and not process anything other than X until
you're on a train to his funeral.
Once there,
they'll remember you for your Blackness.
You never grasped how White they felt,
just focused on the fact that your surname
isn't the same as theirs.
You won't remember their names
but there's not much you
remember from year twelve
and guilt hasn't matured in you. Yet.

You'll be annoyed when sadness doesn't
overwhelm you when your aunt dies.
You'll spend the month before the funeral
trying to logic when the last time
you saw her was. For now,
you'll write the answer down as
twelve years
knowing that you can solve it properly later.
You'll be reminded by the priest
to sit in the family section
for the funeral. Stand next to
your mother as you watch
your cousins bear grief on their shoulders.
You'll catch the purity of pain on their faces
and feel stupid that you tried to
style yours brave.

After the service,
your uncle will stand next to his wife's grave
and tell you of a past you don't remember.
Guilt will let you pay your respects.
It'll only
make itself known on the train ride home.

Everybody Hates Grief

for Dean McKee

For Robin, it's been a struggle.
Constantly gnawing at her,
Grief refuses to leave her alone.
It invited itself to the funeral
even when the rest of her family and friends
couldn't attend and had to watch online.

Abdul has been feeling
lifeless in the living room
ever since Grief cold-called him.
No amount of shielding
was able to protect him from this.

Grief dragged all the words out of
Tyrone's mouth. Left his body numb.
Unable to operate, to feel, to move
for twenty-four hours.
The next day
Tyrone went back to work(ing from home).

Grief visits him in different guises.
Sends him the odd email he wasn't expecting.
Suggests itself on YouTube.
Is a friend he might know on Facebook.
It's a part of Tyrone's life now.
A part he's learning to accommodate.

Sometimes, Grief isn't poetic.

It just hurts

and hurts and hurts.
And during lockdown
it felt like Grief had nowhere else to go
but stay with you.

Grief doesn't observe social distancing.
Doesn't wash its hands.
Doesn't wear a mask.
Sometimes Grief just sucks.

And we go on.
'Cause we have to.

Uniting in memory over loved ones
no longer with us.

Robin and her girls have traded
beer gardens for webcams.
£6 glasses of red have now become
bottles from Tesco.
They drink and share stories of the past.
Have grown to accept virtual hugs
over the real thing.
Allow Grief in on the call but make sure
it keeps its mic muted throughout.

Abdul keeps ordering takeaways
and Amazon deliveries
and as the essential worker that it is
Grief keeps on delivering.
Abdul's coping. He's finding some comfort
in retail therapy over the real thing.

And Tyrone…
Tyrone writes.
Knows Grief only came to visit
after a friend he hadn't seen for two years
was taken from him
and was surprised at how
intrusive Grief was.

Was annoyed that Grief took over his house
until he saw Grief invited over Remembrance.
And, while tales traded over WhatsApp

in lieu of drunken strolls
down memory lane
just don't quite hit right,
they still help us unite.

And sometimes Grief just sucks.

Whenever you lose someone,
of course it will.
You hope it will.
So we take time to remember them.
We need time to remember them.
Time to let Grief… turn into love.
Ensure that their memories live on.
Ensure that we can leave
some memories for others
that'll be worth grieving over.

Ten

1.

I took a huge risk falling for someone like you
        I accidentally burned myself trying to rekindle our old flame
You taught me how wrong my vision of love was
                        I only fell in love with the idea of you
I had dreams about us whilst we became a nightmare
        You taught me why the block button was so important
There's now an 'add friend' button on your Facebook page

2.

                    For lack of a better word, he is my dad
It's just a title. You offer no more than that
                I can't see where he could fit into my life
I've outgrown him, while he wants a part of me
              I still write about him, so maybe I do care…

3.

Rachel should never have got off the plane for Ross
        How I Met Your Mother ended one season sooner. Fact
Vin Diesel is real but Axl Rose is a lie
           The day you accept Taylor Swift, you will know peace
I genuinely believe that Joey and Phoebe could have worked
Scrubs finished on season eight; let's forget season nine happened
It's time that we had the talk. Han shot first
            Pop music is popular for a reason. Just embrace it
Your taste is better than your friends' opinions on it

4.

It's resuscitation. It comes when I am out of air
              Some call it art. I call it a lifestyle choice
I've never stopped loving two things. Words and my mother
           Just give me a chance and I'll create a typhoon
I'm a tidal wave of earthquakes crashing on blank paper
        You're a canvas of ears and eyes, thoughts and hearts
We're fire ice, a dancing helix. We're a kaleidoscope cacophony

Home

When the fire evicts us
and smoke rents out
every room in our house,
when the heat melts the carpets
and the pressure breaks the floorboards,
I'd run back in
and burn for the reception morning where
my mother made us late for school
because Puff Diddy's 'I'll Be Missing You'
was playing
and she had to wait till the song finished
before she could take me.

I'd burn for the night Zach came over
and we were so busy playing with
Buzz and Woody
that my mum forgot to feed me that night.
I'd burn for the
twenty-plus years since
when I never let her forget that,
despite the fact she's always been prepared
to feed me every other day
before and after.

I'd go back and burn
for the Sunday afternoons
after church when Kwabena and Martin
would invite themselves round
and we'd lose hours in *Little Big Planet*
and *Super Sunday* football.

When the fire evicts us
I'd go back in and burn to try and save
every text my mum sent to me
from the living room
whilst I was in my bedroom.
I'd save every 'Put the kettle on' text
she'd send on her way back home
and I'd fight the flames for every look of disappointment on her face
when she got in to no cup of tea.

When the house burns down,
the first things I go back for won't be
the Santa my nan knit me
or my PS5 that my freelancing paid for.
I don't need to save my Venetian masks
or the eight waistcoats in my wardrobe.
I'd just burn for memories.
All the mornings
when I struggled to get out of bed.
I'd burn for every moment,
every raised voice,
every piece of smashed crockery.
I'd burn for it all.

When the house burns down,
when the fire evicts us,
I'd go back in, inhale the smoke,
risk it all to save my mum.
Because when the house becomes ash and dust,
if I save her,
I'll still have a home.

The C Word

She will tell you
that she has her star sign.
You will later tell her
that you'll steal that line
for a poem.
In the moment,
you'll run through every word
she's ever taught you
but not know the right one
to say out loud.
She won't expect you to know.
You'll pay £2 a minute to each
stay in silence
whilst shock eavesdrops in
on the call.

In the moment,
you'll feel every inch of the
3,432 miles between you.
You'll worry that she'll have
to go to sleep alone that night.
She'll be sorry that she's ruined
your work trip away.
She'll wish this might only be
a minor distraction, but you know
everything she does
is major.

She'll have to say it twice.
The lift will cut the sound out
the first time.
When she says it's her star sign
you will know instantly.
We'll both think we could have
handled this moment better.

When the phone call ends
you'll be left on a balcony with
Mortality.
You'll ask them the questions
you forgot to ask her.
Is it benign?
What kind?
What stage?
What next?
What now?

She will tell you
that she has her star sign.
She'll keep saying
she's unwell.
She'll keep saying
she's ill.
She'll keep saying
she's dying.

You'll mistake yourself into
seeing her as healthy.
Trick yourself into thinking
one bread roll a day
now means her appetite is back.

At home, you two will learn to dance.
Charleston, salsa and side-step
all the conversations
you know will need to happen.
Both wishing that if neither of you
says C
then it might not be real.

Go Tell It Over the Hills

Let the records state that
my mother is not a loser.
When they talk about it,
make sure you're aware that
she did not lose her battle with cancer.
This was never a fair fight to begin with.
Cancer blindsided us,
embodied Stone Cold and the Rock,
and BAH GAWD
it brought back the Attitude Era
as it snuck into the ring
whilst the referee was inexplicably knocked out.
Came in carrying an
unidentified foreign object
that some call a steel chair
and struck
and struck
and struck.

Let it be known that
my mother is not a warrior.
The doctors never prescribed her armour.
Never equipped her with a sword and shield.
She was never proficient with the blade.
Doesn't hold martial arts in her DNA.
She may have karate belts in our cupboards
but those moves didn't have the same sticking power
the likes of which riding a bike has.

Let's make it clear that
my mother doesn't know how to ride a bike.
She did not take to swimming like a fish to water.
High school and Duolingo mean she has a
rough grasp on French and Spanish
but fluency is not a skill to ascribe to her.

Let me tell you that
my mother's a runner.
Holds memory of 10ks and marathons
in her legs.
Let her tell you that.
All the time.
Let her show you how seamless it is
to take a conversation about
IKEA furniture
and relate it to running a marathon.
Her body was healthy before.
Used to be part of her routine before.
Was more fluent with Strava than Facebook before.
Four and a half stones ago.

Let me remind you that
my mother loves films.
Attends Odeon like church.
Has worshipped at big screens for decades.
Stayed till the end of the credits of every film
before Marvel made it cool.
Know that she paid attention to
the man behind the curtain.
Was there to watch the flowers come to life
in *ET*.
She watched as Luke and Leia
switched seduction
for siblings.
My mother's *Traded Places* with
the *Village of the Damned*. I've seen her
Get Out to embody the *Black Panther*
and will do so again *The Day After Tomorrow*.

Let me point out
that no matter how many times
I try to put her into words
she simply will not fit.
There is too much of her
to constrict to language.

Too many feelings
far more evolved than English.
The love I have for her is far purer and greater
than the words I have available to me.
There will never be enough poems for her
but I'll be damned if I don't at least
try and close the gap.

Tell it on mountains,
over hills,
everywhere.
Go tell it.
Let the records show
that my mother
is still living.

Acknowledgements

The overlap in the Venn diagram of people who are into poetry and people who are into Roman Reigns and the Bloodline is too small for me to make this whole thing an ACKNOWLEDGE ME bit, but for the four of you in the world that this resonates with... this is for you.

Outside that circle... like with everything I write and everything I do and everything I am... this is for and because of my mum. I acknowledge her as my Tribal Chief.

Kayla Martell Feldman, my chaotic poetry partner in creativity. I acknowledge you.

Monti Rodgers, my book cover artist, my DM and such a great DnD player. As a friend, as an artist, as a warforged, as a human... I acknowledge you.

I got through a lot of people in the first book, so I'm keeping this one simple. I complain a lot about disliking people. And every time I do, every time the world is difficult and I feel like crap, I have so many people in my life who prove that even though, as a whole, the human race kinda sucks, even if the vast majority of the world isn't great... there's still that minority of truly incredible people that I can and do and am lucky to fill my life with. I acknowledge you all.

(Ha, okay, I did make this a Bloodline reference after all! Yay, self-indulgent references.)

Tyrone Lewis
will return

(Or he may not, who knows?)